MONOBLOC

T0327844

MONO BLOC

The Best-Selling Chair of All Time

Hauke Wendler

Designed by
Rutger Fuchs

HATJE
CANTZ

Contents

"A disposable item. Cheapness, banality and ugliness incarnated. A throne of poverty."
Augsburger Allgemeine
"Visual pollution"
Basler Zeitung
"A nightmare made of white plastic"
tip Berlin
"The curse of modernity, at least from an aesthetic point of view."
WDR Radio
"The most hated chair in the world"
Frankfurter Allgemeine Sonntagszeitung

MONOBLOC is the generic name of these plastic chairs that first appeared in the early 1970s—because they are manufactured in one piece and in just one operation, by injection molding.

MONOBLOC chairs are made almost exclusively of polypropylene, a widely used plastic that is also used to make yogurt cups, bottle caps, or bicycle helmets.

Berlin, Germany

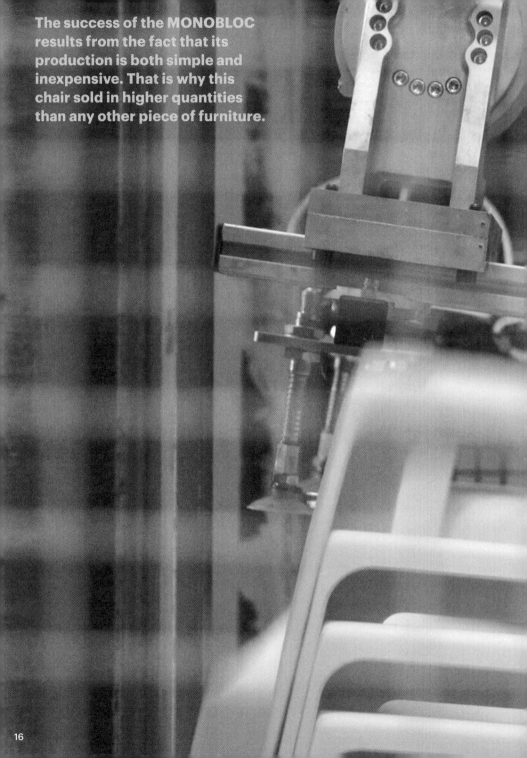

The success of the MONOBLOC results from the fact that its production is both simple and inexpensive. That is why this chair sold in higher quantities than any other piece of furniture.

Jerusalem, Israel
Rio de Janeiro, Brazil

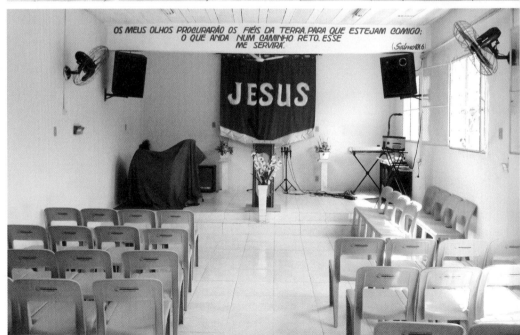

The foundation for the worldwide triumph of the **MONOBLOC** was laid in 1954: it was only with the invention of polypropylene that it became possible to produce chairs that were robust and yet extremely affordable.

San Teodoro, Italy
Istanbul, Turkey

Foreword

Hauke Wendler

At the beginning of a long journey around half the world stood a photograph that had been published in *Die Zeit* in 2013. It showed sixty or seventy of the simple, white plastic chairs that those in the know call the **MONOBLOC**. They were standing in a desert of pebbles and sand, in loose rows, as if the audience had already left. A man with the black-white-and-red flag of Yemen was trudging among them, and the sun cast long shadows over the sea of chairs. A beautiful photograph full of questions and secrets and, at the same time, an unbelievable collection of plastic trash.

That was the starting point of our documentary film about this chair that everyone knows but about which hardly anyone knows anything. This book and a podcast followed, because the **MONOBLOC** wouldn't let go of me. What had initially seemed to be only an absurd, ecologically dubious piece of plastic turned out over the years to be an object with which this world and its order could be narrated and questioned critically.

Perhaps you are thinking that I am exaggerating. But this chair has long been much more than the best-selling piece of furniture of all time, of which there are said to be a billion copies. If you take the time, you will find photographs of the **MONOBLOC** in all conceivable forms, colors, sizes, countries, and social contexts. At first glance, it is a colorful collection of stories, anecdotes, and snapshots. If you look closer, a pattern emerges behind it: the **MONOBLOC** is never standing at the center, never the middle or focus, always at the edge. It is a marginal note made of plastic that nevertheless has its place in the photo albums of human history, and that raises big questions: What is happiness? What does it need in the way of goods, consumption, design—and what doesn't it need?

On the trail of the **MONOBLOC** and its global march of triumph, we traveled five continents, from an industrial region in northern Italy, across Germany, Uganda, the United States, and the megacities of India to a favela in Brazil. The more people we met whose lives were closely tied to this plastic chair, the clearer it became that it is no longer possible to imagine a world without the **MONOBLOC** today. And at the end of that long journey, I am no longer even sure that I would like such a world.

Heute

11.02.2013

Glück gehabt

Die Einsamkeit des Fahnenträgers: Kurz v‹
einer Festveranstaltung zum zweiten Jahre
tag des Beginns des Aufstandes gegen d‹
damaligen Präsidenten des Jemens, Ali A‹
dullah Salih, trägt ein unbekannter Mar
die Landesflagge durch leere Stuhlreih‹
unweit der Hauptstadt Sanaa. Wir könn‹
nur ahnen, was der Mann denkt: War
richtig, Salih Straffreiheit zuzusichern, als
im November 2011 endlich zurücktrat? W
rum steht hier eigentlich überall dieser Pla
tikmüll rum, wo wir doch sonst nichts übr
haben für die Errungenschaften d
Westens? Wo sind die Gäste? Gucken s
lieber die Sendung mit dem Jemen-Wara‹
oder haben wir ihnen allen die jemenitisc‹
Form der Dienstaufsichtsbeschwerde näh‹
gebracht, sie also entführt? Und vor allen
Allah sei Dank, dass Blau nicht das ne‹
Schwarz ist. Sonst trüge ich ja hier die Ho

In a truck converted into an improvised studio, we asked passers-by what they think of MONOBLOC plastic chairs:

"I don't think very highly of plastic chairs; they get shabby over time. I also have a chair on my balcony, but it's made of wicker. Plastic is somewhat hard and not nice, while a wicker chair is always a bit cozy. You sit down and it's warm. This one doesn't get warm at all."

"When you sit on a chair like this for an evening, you never know whether it will hold up. Because it's already happened to me that a leg has broken off while sitting there. That's always a good laugh, but it's also a risk and a game of roulette, a chair like that."

"A chair like that almost cost me my life once. I accidentally sat down a little harder and it broke. I fell on my back and had to go to the hospital. That's why when I see plastic, I see red."

One of the most famous precursors of the basic **MONOBLOC** is the Panton Chair. Since 1958, the Danish designer Verner Panton (1926–1998) published several designs of this classic. It is still being produced today by the Vitra company.

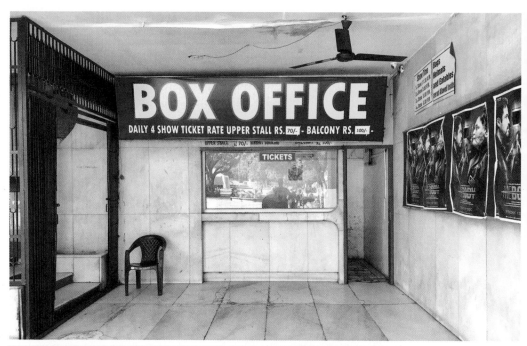

In 1964, German architect and designer Helmut Bätzner (1928–2010) presented the Bofinger chair. Unlike the Panton Chair, it could be stacked and was pressed from polyester. This took about five minutes per chair.

Wilsede, Germany
Kraljevica, Croatia

Three years before Bätzner, the Italian architect and industrial designer Vico Magistretti (1920–2006) had already presented the Selene chair. It has been said of the Italian that he rejected the cheap chairs from the hardware store as "vulgar." But this could not stop the success of the MONOBLOC.

Kigali, Rwanda
Corsica, France

Henry Massonnet (1922–2005) is the inventor of the **MONOBLOC**. In 1948 he founded **STAMP**, the "Societé de Transformation des Matières Plastiques." In 1974 he received an "Oscar du Meuble" for his **MONOBLOC**, which was revolutionary and practical at the same time.

Corsica, France
Pavia, Italy

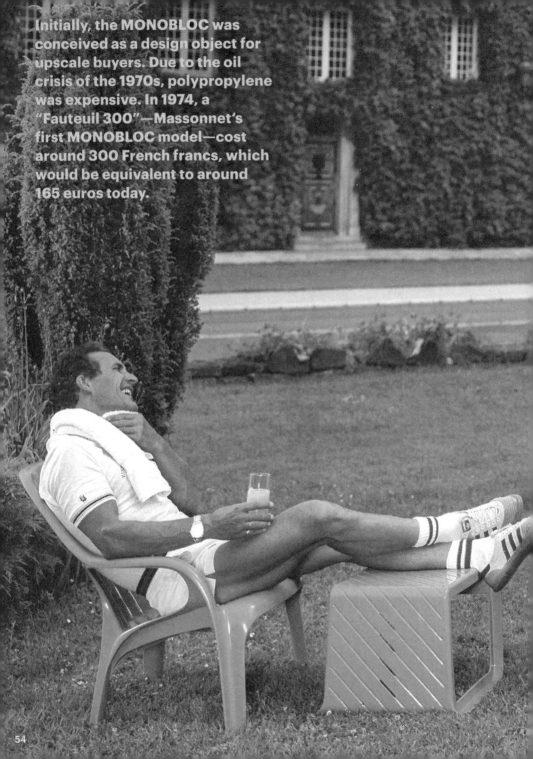

Initially, the **MONOBLOC** was conceived as a design object for upscale buyers. Due to the oil crisis of the 1970s, polypropylene was expensive. In 1974, a "Fauteuil 300"—Massonnet's first **MONOBLOC** model—cost around 300 French francs, which would be equivalent to around 165 euros today.

Henry Massonnet invented a chair without which hundreds of millions of people would be sitting on the floor—literally. Nevertheless, he was almost forgotten when he died in 2005. There had been no way for him to patent his production process.

Alexandria, Egypt

In 2017, the plastic chair made its way into a German cultural temple. "MONOBLOC – A Chair for the World" was the title of the exhibition at the Vitra Design Museum in Weil am Rhein. It caused a sensation in the media—and also irritation among laypeople.

Weil am Rhein, Germany

Heng Zhi

(Curator, Vitra Design Museum)

"Design is reduced by many to beautification; the aesthetic aspects are in the limelight. With the MONOBLOC exhibition, we wanted to break down this way of thinking. Because everyday objects often play a greater role in our lives than the classics or icons."

"When you look at the first MONOBLOC by Massonnet, you realize that the manufacturer was trying to give value to this chair. Massonnet wanted to create a lifestyle object with the new plastic technologies at that time."

"The MONOBLOC reflects the light and dark sides of our consumer society. On the one hand, it is at the forefront of rationalization. On the other hand, one has to ask: Where is all this rationalization and efficiency supposed to take our society?"

Mateo Kries
(Director, Vitra Design Museum)

"When people criticize the MONOBLOC as a fall from grace because it doesn't meet their idea of quality, design, and aesthetics, you can counter that it is in a line of development with important pieces. There it has its significance, whether one likes it or not."

"If, as a design museum, you only show the undisputed icons, you don't get to the crucial points: where do the opinions diverge?"

"This chair always poses anew the age-old question: what part is played by the criterion of price? If I create such a cheap object, to what extent can I accept compromises in quality? But in return a lot of people can afford it."

This is the core of the debate:
Some say the world needs
the cheap MONOBLOC and
support this view with the
billions of units sold. Others
claim that there must be better
alternatives, but they have so
far failed to prove this.

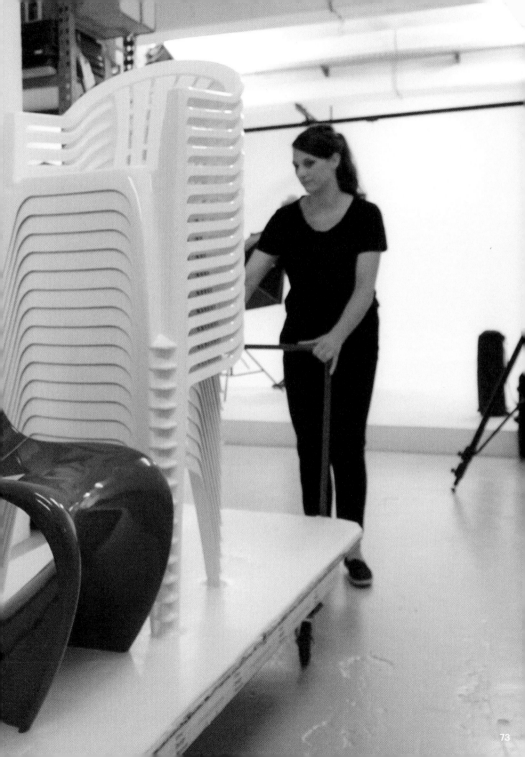

Kolkata, India
Hyderabad, India

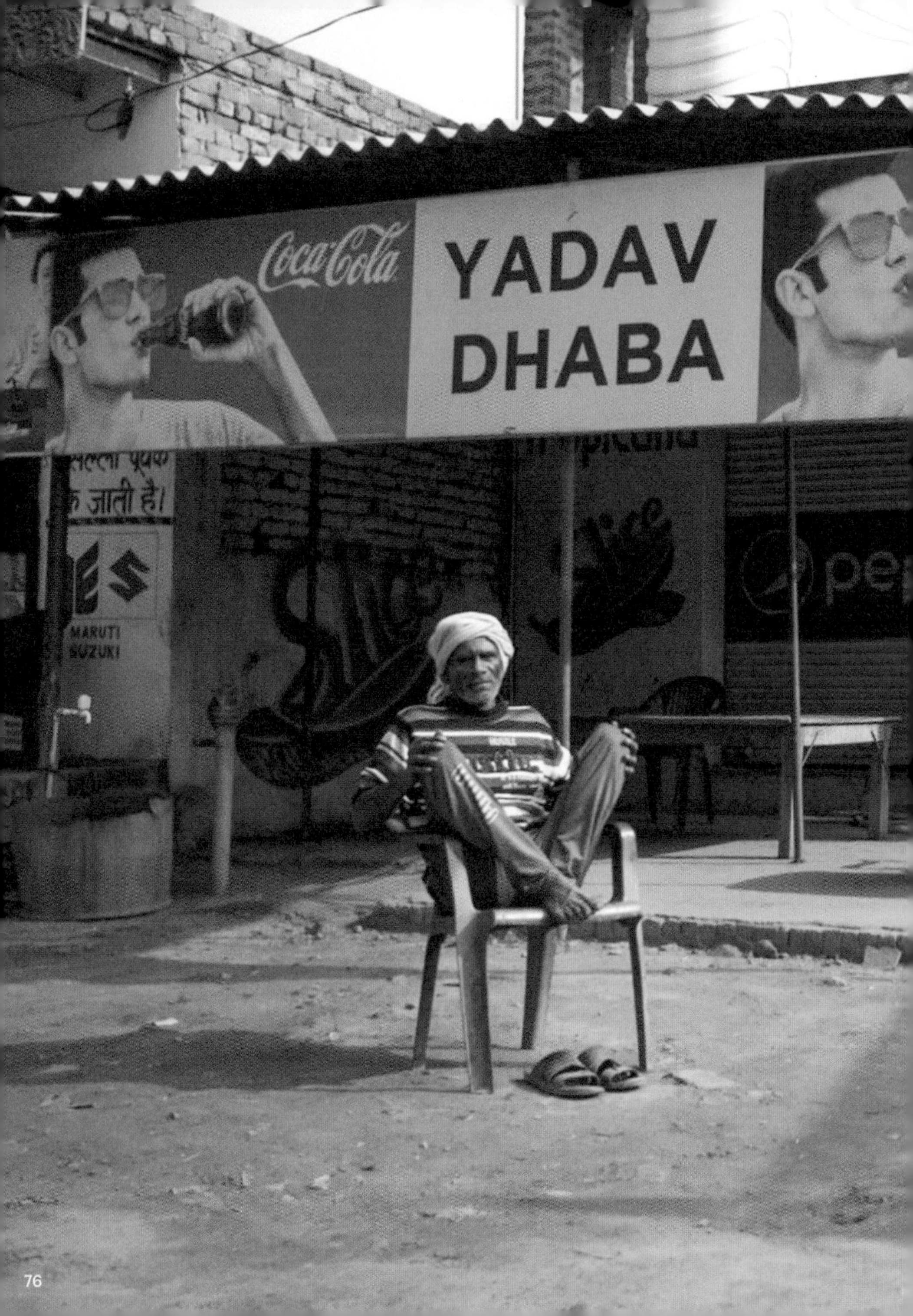
Coca-Cola
YADAV
DHABA
MARUTI
SUZUKI

The MONOBLOC has many practical advantages: it is cheap, so many people can afford it, and it is comparatively easy to manufacture. Experts have therefore described the chair as a "democratic product."

Vientiane, Laos
Mumbai, India

The production of a MONOBLOC takes about one minute. The polypropylene is heated to 220 degrees, and the liquid material is injected into a mold. Then the mold is cooled with water. When it is opened, the MONOBLOC is ready. Ideally, the machines are so precise that nothing needs to be touched up on the finished chair.

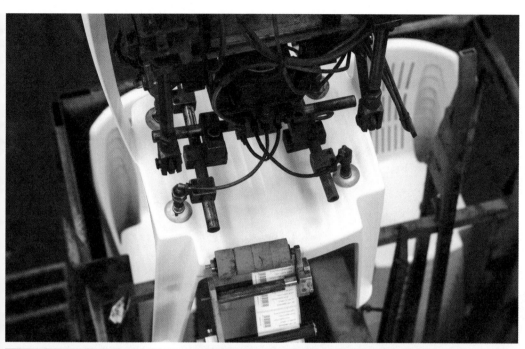

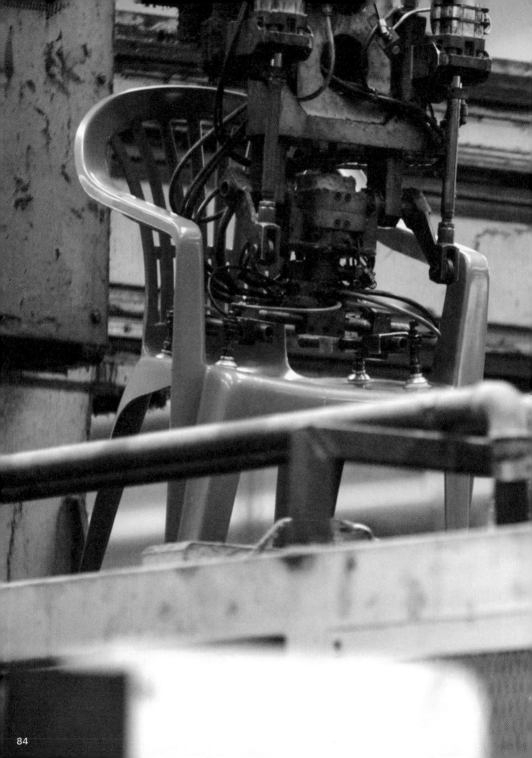

Every 50 to 55 seconds, the robot arm pulls a finished MONOBLOC out of the molding machine. That makes about 60 chairs per hour and a good 1,500 per day per machine.

That's what it is always about with the **MONOBLOC**—money. When the best machine has been bought and the personnel reduced as much as possible, the only thing left to save on is the raw material. That's why every single gram of polypropylene counts.

Sixty years ago in northern Italy, on Lago di Pusiano, one of the first factories for plastic chairs was established. It was founded by Camillo, Carlo, and Serafino Proserpio.

One day a Dutch wholesaler came to the Proserpios. He had a French MONOBLOC with him and said, "If you copy this chair for me, I'll get rid of 10,000 of them." So the three brothers did, and sold 240 million plastic chairs in the following decades.

The Proserpio brothers became involved with the **MONOBLOC** by chance. They copied the idea from others, which was not forbidden—and became rich from the plastic chairs. And with them their whole family.

Carlo Proserpio
(CEO of "ProGarden")

"Some say that the MONOBLOC is to the garden what the Beatles were to music."

"The unique thing about the MONOBLOC is that it is very light and stackable. For us producers who serve an international clientele, this is important because we can fit so many chairs into one truck. Therefore, the transportation costs are very low."

"In order to keep up in the price war for the MONOBLOC, we have to save on the raw material. The less polypropylene we use, the better. Because the cost of the raw material does not depend on us, but on the price of oil."

"We have been fortunate to be among the first to produce the MONOBLOC. And we have had great success."

Camillo Proserpio (1931–2018)

(Founder of "ProGarden")

"At the beginning, we only wanted to produce casting and injection molds. Then I made a mold for a company in Milan. That was the first time I saw how plastic was processed. Then, in 1965, we started working with plastic ourselves."

"The MONOBLOC was a chair that really had an impact on the market. Because it was cheap, there was a huge demand in the 1980s. That was the time when plastic was booming, and that's where we got in."

"What is the secret of life? You have to have a little luck. And I had my two brothers. At the end of the day, we have always remained a family of hard-working people."

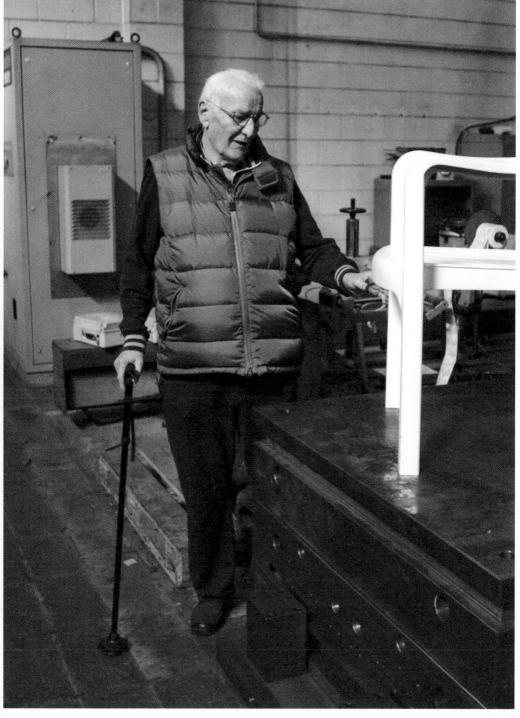

The computer-controlled milling machine is used to carve out the mold of a MONOBLOC from a block of stainless steel, which is very time-consuming and expensive. When the molds are worn out, wholesalers sell them to Africa, Asia, or South America. There they are used for years to produce chairs that are not of such high quality.

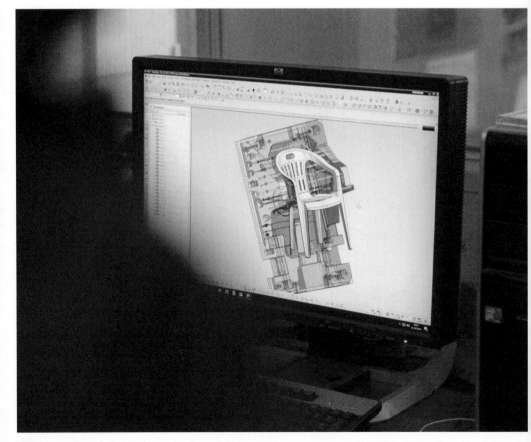

There are seventy million people worldwide who need a wheelchair but do not have enough money. For these women and men, the charity "Free Wheelchair Mission" has developed the "Gen One": the world's cheapest wheelchair, a MONOBLOC on wheels.

Annet Nnabulime
(Former shopkeeper)

"In the beginning, five years ago, I was just suffering from back pain. Then, suddenly, I was paralyzed. At that time everything collapsed, my life, my work. I had no hope anymore."

"Before that I had work at the lake, I had a store there. That's how I paid the children's school fees. I have many children, including adopted ones. But then I got sick and my family was destroyed because I couldn't work anymore. The problem is that my husband died a long time ago."

"I'm really happy about the wheelchair. It was always really bad when it was raining. Because I had to drag myself along the ground. Now I can go everywhere. It makes everything a lot easier."

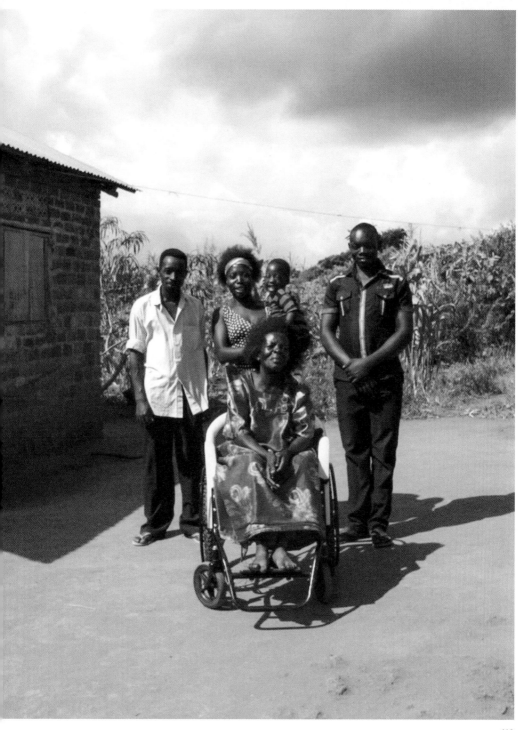

Los Angeles, USA
Corsica, France

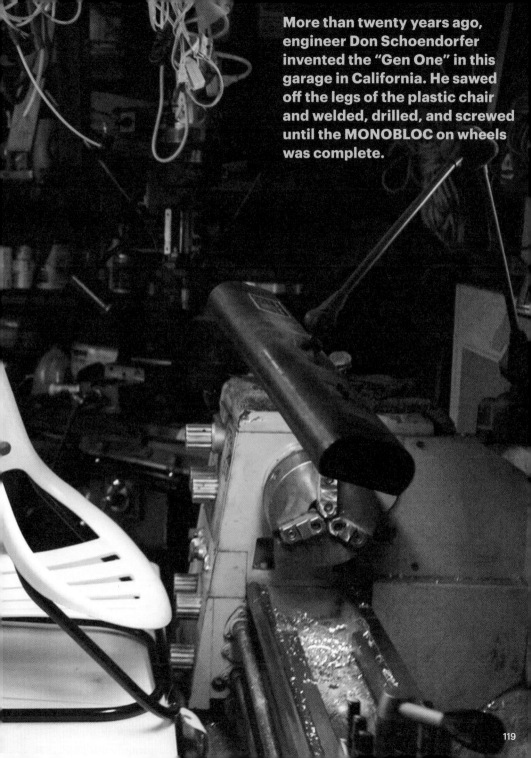

More than twenty years ago, engineer Don Schoendorfer invented the "Gen One" in this garage in California. He sawed off the legs of the plastic chair and welded, drilled, and screwed until the MONOBLOC on wheels was complete.

To date, "Free Wheelchair Mission" has distributed 1.2 million wheelchairs in ninety-four countries worldwide. The goal is to reach two million by 2025. The Christian mission organization in the USA is financed by donations.

Don Schoendorfer

(Founder of "Free Wheelchair Mission")

"It's almost like the people in the developing world get leftovers. They get used clothing, they get surplus food that no one else wants. No one ever comes around and says: We can do better than that."

"I went to the local mall and looked up what each component would cost. I thought about building a wheelchair for thirty dollars. That was the goal."

"We started out just trying to come up with the least expensive, most durable wheelchair we could make. I needed to get the cost down as much as possible, so that is when the engineering came in view, and what is the most common chair in the world? The MONOBLOC."

Francis Mugwanya

(Founder and Director of "Father's Heart Mobility Ministry")

"I was born like any other normal child. But when I was three and a half years old I got polio. Because of what I went through as a child, I run the 'Father's Heart Mobility Ministry' to distribute wheelchairs to people who cannot afford them."

"In Uganda it is estimated that we have about five million people with different forms of disabilities. Our population now is about forty million, so five million is a lot. And among those, one million are expected to need but not have wheelchairs."

"People would criticize a 'Gen One' and say: Why don't we give them a better one? Well, if you cannot afford a wheelchair, would you rather wait until you have saved 2,000 dollars, or would you rather be off the ground with a 'Gen One' with a plastic chair in it?"

"In Uganda, a plastic chair is not a joke. A plastic chair is one that is meeting a practical need."

Fortaleza, Brazil

At the end of the 1990s, criticism of the MONOBLOC grew louder. In Copenhagen, Freiburg, Palma de Mallorca, and other cities, a ban was discussed. Bern and Basel even made it illegal to use the chair in their city centers.

Detfurth, Germany

In countries like India, where the majority of the population lives on the poverty line, there have been no such debates. There, you can hardly find a street corner without plastic chairs.

As the market for plastic chairs grew, a fierce price war broke out among manufacturers in India. More and more money was saved on the material—at the expense of the quality of **MONOBLOC** chairs—just like everywhere else in the world.

Because some machines or molds used in India are not as high quality as those used in Europe, liquid plastic sometimes leaks out and forms so-called "fish skins." These are removed by hand before sale.

Sanjeev Jain

(Vice-President of the furniture division, "Supreme Industries")

"'Supreme Industries' is one of the largest plastic processing companies in India. With the MONOBLOC chair, we started in 1990. Looking back, generally, people would not have any dining seating in their homes. Those at a lower middle class income would sit on the floor. But today, because of plastic furniture, this is different."

"I have heard of criticism in Europe about plastic chairs. Europe has a very developed economy, so people can afford to buy an expensive product. But that does not mean that people who cannot afford to do this should not buy a plastic chair."

"We have had the discussion many time: Should we do away with plastic or not? But 'Supreme Industries' has stayed with plastic because we still believe that plastic is a product to stay."

Harnack Singh

(Foreman, "Supreme Industries")

"I was incredibly fortunate to get this job.
I started here as a laborer. Now I'm in charge
of more than twelve machines. It enables me
to give my children a better future. If I was a
farmer, I could not afford a good school for
them. I work with plastic chairs. But we have
been farming the land for generations."

"It is true that plastic is not good for the
environment. But plastic chairs are beneficial
to all of us. Plastic is needed everywhere,
throughout the whole country."

Lalru, India

"Supreme Industries" has developed a new, technically advanced generation of MONOBLOC chairs, as recently offered by European manufacturers in a similar form. The aim is to win back customers from the middle class.

"The disposal of the chair is an ecological disaster. It is lying around everywhere, on the field, in the forest, river and sea, unbreakable and non-decomposable."

"For me, the chair is one of these disposable items that do not belong in our culture and our civilization."

Hamburg, Germany

(1st lady, right) "I thought those were retired a long time ago."

(2nd lady, left) "They should be recycled. But they probably can't even be recycled, right? That's the problem."

(Man) "When I want to pick out a nice piece of furniture for our backyard, ninety percent of the time I'm faced with plastic first."

The collaborative "Rosa Virginia" is an association of women from a favela near Fortaleza in Brazil. Men are the exception here. They collect fifty-two different recyclable materials, mainly metal, paper, cardboard, and plastic.

Maria Ilda de Andrade

(Garbage collector)

"I have a very small house and get by with recycling. I used to get no money at all, working for a family in the household. Now I'm doing better because I earn some money regularly."

"In a month, I have 200 to 300 reais (about 40 to 60 euros). If I find a plastic chair, that's great! I earn four reais (85 cents) from that alone. The other things—PET, plastic wrap, cardboard—bring in less than a chair."

"I am not ashamed of my work. You only have to be ashamed when you steal something, not when you take something. I take things from the trash so that I have something for living."

Musamara Mendes Pereira

(Collaborative "Rosa Virginia")

"People think: What's not important to me is garbage. They throw it away because it is worthless to them. Then the garbage collector comes along and finds value in it. And his livelihood."

"Wherever a lot of people gather, you'll find plastic chairs. For waste collectors, of course, this is great. Because polypropylene is a material that fetches a very good price when recycled."

"Those who have to collect garbage often feel inferior. They all felt ashamed. So we decided to rent a house to collect the garbage together and sell it. That way, we get more out of it."

Petra, Jordan
Pushkar, India

In Brazil, you can find companies everywhere that recycle old plastic chairs. Because it is profitable to recycle the polypropylene. With every truck, hundreds of broken chairs end up here, chopped up by workers with machetes.

In a shed, the plastic parts are ground up and washed. It is noisy, the air is dusty. Recycling is important, but it also has its downsides: working conditions in factories like this are very tough.

Ary Jaime De Albuquerque

(Founder of "Indústria Brasileira de Artefatos Plásticos")

"The recycling company processes the old polypropylene into a granulate that they sell to us. My company has been working with recycled material for fifty years now. Back then, we started doing it because there was simply not enough raw material in Brazil."

"I think that we should recycle as much as possible in the world. Recycling is the only right way. Not just for us, but for all of humanity, all over the world."

"We live in a country that has yet to develop. In Europe there is a lot of money, the consumption of plastic is much lower there. Here, plastic dominates every city, every favela. When you walk across the street, everything is full of plastic."

New **MONOBLOC** chairs are created from the polypropylene recovered during recycling. They are inferior to their predecessors, but they are sold at an even lower price.

Moss, Norway
Castillo de San Felipe, Guatemala

"I started working here after school. Panel beating and paint jobs. When a customer arrives, we have to offer him the chair. The customer relaxes while we carry out the work. Once the customer has left, we go back to sitting on the chair to relax. It is much more relaxing to sit on the chair than on the floor."

"My father founded this business in 1967. Back then, it was steel-tube garden furniture. This lasted until 1975. After that, we sold wooden furniture. And then, in 1985, foreign companies introduced plastic molded furniture. It was a huge success."

Kurukshetra, India
New Delhi, India

"I founded my company in 2008. We sell tankers. At that time I had two employees, today there are fifty-five. But I have always kept the chairs because they are comfortable. Every day I sit here with friends and drink tea."

"This is a nursery. I sell plants. I'm the owner. We have a lot of pollution here. That is why I like to sit among the plants, on the chair."

"Every morning I open my store and sweep first. Then I sit down on the chair and wait for customers. The plastic chair is all I need. Because the store is small, I couldn't afford another one."

"I am a timber merchant. I have fourteen people working for me. I have had this chair for many years. Once a beam fell on it, and after that it had to be repaired, that is, sewn. That's why I particularly like this plastic chair."

"I work on the sidewalk because I cannot afford a store. The store owner rents me the space here. The plastic chairs are his. That is where his customers and mine are sitting. The wooden chairs before were not as good."

"I attend Sunlight Elementary School and am in the fifth grade. With the store here, I can earn a little extra for my school fees. I fetch water and clean the chairs."

Afterword
Hauke Wendler

When our project began, the MONOBLOC was, for me too, just a banal, absurd object. Today, eight years later, I am embarrassed by the arrogance with which we in the West often regard the rest of humanity.

While working on my film and this book, I got to know the impressive women and men who live with or from this plastic chair in Uganda, India, and Brazil, among other places. For me, that was a turning point. Suddenly the owners of this chair had faces: that of Annet Nnabulime in Uganda and of Harnack Singh in India and of Maria Ilda de Andrade in a favela near Fortaleza. Do we want to continue to mock the only chair these people can afford? A chair that is quite practical and recyclable to boot?

The MONOBLOC is still not my favorite item of furniture. I am pleased that other chairs are standing in our kitchen, living room, and office. But millions of people in our world depend on precisely this model, because they have no alternative. And what counts in the end is not the chair but that they are sitting.

Winter 2021–22

Colophon

Managing editors
Hauke Wendler, Rutger Fuchs,
Nicola von Velsen

Project management
Carina Bukuts, Fabian Reichel

Proofreading
Diane Fortenberry

Graphic design
Rutger Fuchs

Production
Thomas Lemaître

Reproductions
DLG Graphics, Paris

Printing
Livonia Print Ltd.

Paper
Munken Print White, 115 g/m²

Typeface
Graphik

**© 2022 Hatje Cantz Verlag,
Berlin, and Hauke Wendler
© for the images: The
photographers according
to credits**

This book is published
in conjunction with the
documentary of the same
name by Hauke Wendler
and Pier 53.

Image credits
Cover and dustjacket, pp. 6–7:
Andreas Sütterlin

p. 8: Stephan Pramme

pp. 9t, 12, 22t, 23t, 40b, 44b,
48t, 49, 70, 71, 86, 87, 90b, 94,
95, 115b, 132, 133, 137t, 164t,
165, 177t: cc-by Henning Wötzel-
Herber

p. 9b: cc-by Annette Ullrich,
curated by Henning Wötzel-
Herber

pp. 10–11, 14–15, 16–17, 24–25, 33,
34, 36–37, 58–59, 62–63, 64, 65,
67, 69, 72–73, 76–77, 80–81, 82,
83, 84–85, 88–89, 92–93, 96–97,
100–101, 103, 105, 106–107,
108, 109, 116–117, 118–119, 120,
121u, 125, 127, 128–129, 134–135,
138–139, 142–143, 145, 147, 148,
149, 150–151, 153, 154, 156–157,
161, 162–163, 166–167, 170–171,
173, 174–175, 178–179, 181, 182,
185, 186, 188–189: Boris Mahlau /
Pier 53

p. 13: cc-by Anica Richter,
curated by Henning Wötzel-
Herber

p. 18t: cc-by Ondřej Žváček

pp. 18b, 19, 20–21, 22b: Stephan
Lanz

p. 23b: cc-by Antonia Saldinger,
curated by Henning Wötzel-
Herber

pp. 29t, 40t, 48b, 52, 113, 114,
115t, 121t, 130–131, 137b, 159:
Hauke Wendler

p. 29b: Jonny Müller-
Goldenstedt / Pier 53

pp. 30–31: *Die Zeit*, February 2,
2013

pp. 38–39: Cover *Mobilia
Magazine* No. 145 (1967)

p. 41: cc-by Eike Rösch, curated
by Henning Wötzel-Herber

pp. 42–43: Alexandra Alge

p. 44t: Andrea Pittlik

pp. 45, 60, 61, 74, 79, 90t, 99b,
136, 140, 141, 168, 169: Volker
Albus

pp. 46–47: Kooloo Modern

pp. 50–51, 54–55, 56, 57:
Advertising brochure STAMP
(1972)

p. 53: cc-by Renata Buchholz,
curated by Henning Wötzel-
Herber

pp. 75, 177b: Rutger Fuchs

p. 78t: Katrin Mersmann

pp. 78b, 164b: cc-by Birte Frische,
curated by Henning Wötzel-
Herber

p. 91: cc-by Steph Baltes, curated
by Henning Wötzel-Herber

p. 98: cc-by Tariq Muman, curated
by Henning Wötzel-Herber

p. 99t: cc-by Anand Madhvan,
curated by Henning Wötzel-
Herber

pp. 110–111, 122–123: Free
Wheelchair Mission

p. 176t: cc-by Thomas Nielsen,
curated by Henning Wötzel-
Herber

p. 176b: cc-by Paul van Oss,
curated by Henning Wötzel-
Herber

The publisher and author have
made every effort to research
all copyrights to third-party
images and to indicate them
accurately. If this has not been
done in individual cases, please
contact us.

**Published by
Hatje Cantz Verlag GmbH
Mommsenstraße 27
10629 Berlin
www.hatjecantz.com**
A Ganske Publishing Group
Company

ISBN
978-3-7757-5191-9
Printed in Latvia